NON-ALCOHOLIC COCKTAILS

-MOCKTAILS
-SMOOTHIES
-MILKSHAKES

LA MIA PASSIONE
RACCONTATA ATTRAVERSO I DRINK FATTI DA ME E BEVUTI DA VOI

This manual was written with the intention of giving a complete overview of the vast world of non-alcoholic cocktails.

Alcohol-free drinks are often seen, especially in the menus of many places, as lower category drinks and not much space is dedicated to them; on the other hand, with the passing of the years, habits, lifestyle and even laws change, are more and more requested and known.

The aim of this manual is therefore to help readers find and create, using a pinch of their imagination, modern non-alcoholic cocktails with not only visual but also taste impact.

MOCKTAILS

Defining mocktails simply as alcohol-free cocktails would be really unfair and would mean belittling both the material and intellectual work that allowed their creation. Non-alcoholic cocktails are now depopulated in the most famous clubs of the bartending capitals from New York to London have nothing to envy to the classic drinks based on gin, whiskey or rum even if of course in some cases they are inspired by them.

At one time, alcohol-free cocktails like Shirley Temple and Virgin Mojito were found on the last pages of the drinks lists of American bars, lounge bars, pubs and restaurants, usually ordered only by children, teetotalers and drivers designated by the group of friends to bring back, rightly so , all home safe and sound. Today, on the other hand, mocktails have ceased to be less appropriate alternatives to the great international drinks, and are a rapidly growing market segment and an idea to try even at home since the ingredients are often already in our kitchens.

In recent years, the culture of drinking has considerably evolved and cocktails enthusiasts have rapidly increased not only in number, but also and above all in their awareness as an informed consumer to safeguard their palate and health.

For this reason, customers appreciate and go in search of more sophisticated ingredients, the balance and balance of flavors and aromas, just like sommeliers do to choose a wine suitable for the occasion; in fact, with always new and numerous recipes designed for specific moments, which in addition to the classic between meals meet the combination with food and even the daytime hours of the day, cocktails have invaded our days, dinners, lunches, brunches independently by their more or less alcoholic content.

The new trend of international mixology therefore aims to reduce the alcohol content of cocktails more and more, whether they are for aperitifs, after dinner, or as a meal.

The absence of alcohol is no longer the only main feature of mocktails, today the focus is on the quality and combination of the ingredients present in this type of drink. They are no longer "without" versions, but recipes built, conceived and designed for different moments of the day and different occasions of use, "with", so much to offer and for the public to discover ".

Today, mocktails are so popular that the trendiest places have recipes "of the house" dedicated to individual moments of the day, from aperitifs to after dinner, and above all to new occasions such as brunches and lunches, once off-limits times for bartenders. In Milan, two of the cocktails that are having the most success in the places where we studied the drink list, are just two mocktails and are drunk during the day or at mealtimes. Acqua di mare is a cocktail based on Mediterranean water, lemon juice, black pepper sugar syrup and soda, very popular, as much as Profumi di Campo, based on rosemary syrup, cucumber extract and lime juice ".

Cocktails have become seasonal, like cooking, you no longer drink the same things all year round, apart from the indisputable personal tastes and the great classics that cannot and should not be eliminated from the menu.

The cocktail bars change their lists every season, like the restaurants, just to be inspired by different ingredients and flavors. Now in winter, spicy and red fruit notes are preferred, which recall those typical of Christmas. There is no limit to the imagination "because the barmen are no longer satisfied with the products on the market and how chefs prepare their own syrups, extracts and many infusions with which to" cook "cocktails on the spot" concludes Alessandro. Using the infusions Pompadour has created six cocktails exclusively for Italian cuisine, such as Cinnamon Red, based on Carnation and Cinnamon Infusion and many other recipes.

If we wanted to give a concise definition of these drinks we could describe them as follows:

"MOCKTAILS ARE ORIGINAL AND ALCOHOL-FREE MIXTURES, FRUIT OF THE BARTENDER'S EXTRACTION AND CREATIVITY".

A curious topic to address is certainly where the term mocktail comes from: in cinematic jargon the mockumentary is a genre of fiction that follows the style and language of the documentary. The word is the crasis of two terms: documentary merges with mock, that is fake and, if used as a verb, it means to make fun or make a verse. The same mechanism is applied to the word mocktail which indicates reinterpretations of classic cocktails or original mixes but strictly alcohol-free. In the food sector, as already pointed out, the attention towards different tastes, choices or needs is growing. It is also true that in recent years, one of the biggest trends has certainly been the re-discovery of quality mixology: increasingly balanced drinks, designed by whimsical bartenders, who use juices, homemade tinctures and bitters with fine spirits The combination of these two trends has led to the expansion of the offer of non-alcoholic alternatives. Finally, even abstainers and those who, even temporarily, want or need to avoid alcohol, can drink something interesting and test the skill of a barman. It is not just a matter of re-proposing cocktails deprived of the alcoholic component but of resorting to creativity, to find the right combination of natural ingredients, in order to overcome even the use of carbonated drinks, syrups rich in sugars or industrial fruit juices. they want or need to avoid alcohol, they can drink something interesting and test the skill of a bartender. It is not just a matter of re-proposing cocktails deprived of the alcoholic component but of resorting to creativity, to find the right combination of natural ingredients, in order to overcome even the use of carbonated drinks, syrups rich in sugars or industrial fruit juices. they want or need to avoid alcohol, they can drink something interesting and test the skill of a bartender. It is not just a matter of re-proposing cocktails deprived of the alcoholic component but of resorting to creativity, to find the right combination of natural ingredients, in order to overcome even the use of carbonated drinks, syrups rich in sugars or industrial fruit juices.

In short, the days of Paradise, San Francisco or Virgin Colada are over, current customers are not satisfied with limiting their alcohol intake but aim for cocktails that must even be healthy, with detox, energizing or slimming variants (alcohol it is one of the components that makes you fat the most when drinking and combined with sugar or fruit it can become the worst enemy of your figure and body health).

Fruit certainly remains the absolute protagonist: citrus fruits, pineapple but also blueberries and pomegranate, to be added perhaps to carrots, celery, mint, cucumbers, basil, chia seeds and almonds; unmissable jokers are turmeric and ginger, whose properties seem endless. Great popularity also for coconut water and green tea which often represent the basis of blending.

Beyond the purely healthy aspect, the point of view of those who find themselves dealing with when pairing with food comes into play is interesting. We inevitably start with a void to fill in terms of acidity, fullness of the body and a sensation of heat, especially when it comes to coping with the complexity of some recipes. So there are two ways: to find solutions with certain ingredients capable of providing an aromatic profile and mouthful sensations such as to make up for the absence of alcohol (algae, chilli, aromatic herbs) or to recreate the organoleptic sensations of traditional cocktails or even of great wines. , in a soft drink.

For all these reasons, the fashion of mocktails has become increasingly popular also in Italy.

This trend certainly has the merit of stimulating the workers in the sector, forced, as during prohibition, to rediscover certain ingredients or at least to re-evaluate their use. The domino effect that started from the cocktail bar counters inevitably also involved the kitchens of important restaurants and not only in the United States but also in Australia and Great Britain. To understand the state of things in Italy it is useful to look at the experience of the Road Safety Week of May 2015, with a Michelin license plate. The 39 Italian chefs with two or three stars were asked to prepare a menu dedicated to the theme and, of course, the question of reducing alcohol was absolutely central. The only one to propose what we could call a mocktail was Moreno Cedroni with an energy drink based on lime and ginger. Davide Scabin, on the other hand, deserves the credit for having thought of an entire pairing process, with natural juices and nectars. Everyone else practically limited themselves to recommending drinking in moderation. The market responds with enthusiasm to this new trend and, apart from the public utterances of Gualtiero Marchesi, who claims he hasn't touched alcohol for about 20 years, even in private some great chefs have admitted to taking a certain pleasure in playing with drinks. non-alcoholic.

MOCKTAILS RECIPES YOU MUST TRY

LEMON AND LAVENDER MOCKTAIL

Ingredients:

60 ml of lemon juice,
25 ml of lavender syrup,
3.5 ml of grenadine,
3 drops of bitters.

Preparation:

Put all the ingredients in a shaker with ice and shake until it becomes cold. Garnish with fresh lavender. To make it turn lavender, add very little blue food coloring with the tip of a toothpick.

FRENCH 75 MOCKTAIL

Ingredients:

90 ml of lemon juice,
4 sprinkles of lemon or orange bitters, 200 g of excellent tonic water,
2 cocktail sticks of sugar, ice.

Preparation:

Put the lemon juice and the bitter in a shaker filled with ice. Shake until frozen, then divide into two champagne flutes. Fill with tonic water until it reaches 3/4 of the glass. Garnish with cocktail sticks and serve immediately.

MINT AND RASPBERRY LEMONADE

Ingredients:

300 gr of raspberries,
360 ml of water,
55 grams of brown sugar,
8 mint leaves (plus more for garnish),

240 ml of freshly squeezed lime juice, 720 ml of soda.

Preparation:

Place the raspberries, water and sugar in a high-sided pan and bring to a boil over medium-high heat. Lower the heat and simmer for 5 minutes, stirring occasionally, until the raspberries are soft and almost dissolved. Add the mint leaves, then remove from the heat and allow to cool, then remove the mint. For a thicker drink, blend everything with an immersion blender. For a lighter drink, filter, thus eliminating all the solid part. Add the lime juice, Divide the mixture into 6 glasses, then fill them with soda, garnish with fresh mint leaves and serve.

CRANBERRY AND LIME MOCKTAIL

Ingredients:

two packs of fresh cranberries,
240 ml of water,
200 grams of sugar,
350 gr of sparkling lemonade (preferably with lime),
cranberry syrup.

Preparation:

For the blueberry syrup. Blend the blueberries until they are completely chopped. Then put the blueberries, water and sugar in a pan and cook over medium heat until the sugar has dissolved (about two minutes). Strain the mixture to remove the solid part and set aside. For the mocktail. Fill two very high-sided glasses with ice, add two tablespoons of blueberry syrup to each glass, then fill with sparkling lemonade. Garnish to taste with frozen cranberries and lime wedges.

MOCKTAIL ALLA SANGRIA

Ingredients:

1 liter of white grape juice,
40 gr + 120 gr of blueberries,
250 ml of orange juice,
the juice of 1 lime + 2 limes, 2 oranges, 2 bananas, 2 peaches.

Preparation:

Blend the grape juice with 40 g of blueberries. Add the orange juice and lime juice and mix. Put everything in a large bowl, adding ice, the chopped fruit and the remaining blueberries. Leave the sangria to rest for at least 2 hours in the fridge, then serve.

MORNING MOCKTAIL

Ingredients:

frozen orange juice cubes,
240 ml of sparkling water,
a splash of grenadine,
a sprig of rosemary,
a splash of vanilla syrup (optional).

Preparation:
Place two balls of frozen orange juice in a glass. Add the sparkling water. Slowly pour in the grenadine and vanilla syrup. Serve with a sprig of rosemary.

GRAPEFRUIT, GINGER AND BASIL MOCKTAIL

Ingredients:

1 grapefruit (plus more for garnish),
3 350g packs of ginger soda, a handful of fresh basil,
60 ml of basil syrup.

For the basil syrup: 200 g of sugar, 240 ml of water, a package of fresh basil.

Preparation:

For the basil syrup. Put the sugar and water in a small skillet over medium heat, until the sugar has dissolved completely (about two minutes). Add the basil and leave it to infuse for 15-20 minutes. Remove the basil and set aside.

For the mocktail. Squeeze the grapefruit, Fill a jug with ice and pour the ginger soda, grapefruit juice and basil syrup and mix well. Garnish with grapefruit slices and fresh basil leaves.

APPLE MOCKTAIL

Ingredients:

275 gr of apple juice,
a pack of frozen cranberry juice,
1 liter of sparkling soda,
240 ml of orange juice.

Preparation:

Mix all the ingredients well and garnish with apple slices to taste.

BLUEBERRY LEMONADE AND BOURBON VANILLA

Ingredients:

30 ml of freshly squeezed lemon juice, 2 gr of bourbon vanilla,
5-10 ml of simple syrup,
half a bottle of blueberry soda,
crushed ice, blueberries.

Preparation:

At the base of a high-sided glass, put the lemon juice, vanilla, syrup, some blueberries and mix. Add a generous amount of crushed ice, fill with soda and mix. Garnish with a slice of lemon.

ORANGE EGGNOG MOCKTAIL

Ingredients:

a pack of 175 grams of concentrated orange juice,
240 ml of ready-made eggnog without alcohol, 240 ml of water,
a teaspoon of vanilla,
70 grams of sugar,
a pinch of grated nutmeg, ice, whipped cream.

Preparation:

Put all the ingredients in a blender, starting from the eggnog and the water. Blend on high speed for 2 minutes. Put the mixture in the glasses and garnish with whipped cream and nutmeg.

RED MOON

Ready in 5 minutes
Serve in a whiskey glass

Ingredients:

180 ml of carbonated water
60 ml of plum-cinnamon shrub
plum slices to decorate

Preparation:

Mix the shrub with the carbonated water in a glass filled with ice and mix well. Garnish with plum slices.

THAI MANGO ICE TEA

Ready in 5 minutes, plus 10 minutes of cooling - Serve in a tumbler

Ingredients:

2 teaspoons of cashew drink
2 teaspoons of condensed milk
2 teaspoons of granulated sugar
½ teaspoon of molasses
1 bag of Thai black tea
240 ml of boiling water
4 slices of dehydrated mango and a few more cut into thin strips to decorate

Preparation:

In a large cup or bowl, steep the tea, mango and sugar in hot water, then allow to cool. Remove the mango and the tea bag. Add the remaining ingredients and mix. Serve in a large glass filled with ice cubes and garnish with the thin mango strips.

SUN COCKTAIL

Ready in 5 minutes
Serve in a tumbler

Ingredients:

1 sprig of mint and a lime wedge to decorate
60 ml of lime juice
½ teaspoon of molasses
240 ml of ginger soda

Preparation:

In a large glass filled with crushed ice, mix all the ingredients, pouring in the molasses first, then the ginger soda and finally the lime juice. Garnish with the lime wedge and mint.

MOJITO

Ready in 5 minutes
Serve in a whiskey glass

Ingredients:

200 ml of ginger soda
30 ml of lime juice
30 ml of simple syrup
10 mint leaves and some sprig to decorate
1 lime wedge to decorate

Preparation:

Press the mint leaves in a shaker, add the syrup and lime juice, then some ice and shake well. Top with ginger soda, then strain and serve in a glass filled with ice. Garnish with a sprig of mint and a wedge of lime.

OTHER 15 DELICIOUS RECIPES WITH MORE PARTICULAR INGREDIENTS.

TRINI TEA

If you're looking to pamper yourself with something warm and sweet with a hint of citrus, the Trini Tea mocktail by Angostura Aromatic Bitters is the right choice.

ingredients:

9 cl coffee
4.5 cl coconut milk
1,5 cl cascara tea syrup
Aromatic macaroons
Angostura bitter orange

Preparation:

Pour the two hot cups of coffee into the shaker together with all the other ingredients, shake vigorously and serve in a teacup to keep the heat at its best.

HONEYCRISP COOLER

This sweet and refreshing mocktail offers the thirst-quenching taste of apples with a hint of lemon. The addition of a little ginger syrup gives the cocktail a well-rounded flavor profile that makes sipping this drink tasty.

Ingredients:
6 cl Honeycrisp fresh apple juice
1,5 cl ginger syrup *
1,5 cl fresh lemon juice
9 cl Tonic Water
apple slice for garnish

* Ginger Syrup Ingredients: (1 cup of water, 1 cup of granulated sugar
a 2-inch piece of ginger, peeled and thinly sliced

Preparation:

Add all the ingredients to a serving glass with ice.
Mix, garnish with an apple slice and serve.

Preparation of ginger syrup:

Combine the water and ginger in a pan. Bring to the boil.
Once boiling, stir the sugar slowly until completely dissolved.
Reduce the heat. Boil for 20 minutes.
Let it cool down. Filter the ginger before use.

PINEAPPLE RAMOS

If during the cold winter months you miss your last vacation in the tropics, Ananas Ramos will bring you back. This creamy mix of flavors is an ideal way to get into the spirit of the island.

Ingredients:

9 cl pineapple juice
6 cl heavy cream
3 cl lemon juice
3 cl simple syrup *
10 drops of vanilla extract
1 egg white
1 can of carbonated water
pineapple wedge for garnish

Preparation:

Mix all the ingredients except the soda water. Shake once without ice and once with ice.
Pour into a glass with 9 cl of seltzer water.
Garnish with a slice of pineapple and add a straw.

* Mix equal volumes of sugar and boiling water. Stir until dissolved and let cool.

JET SET

This refreshing and aromatic mocktail brings a bit of an herb garden into your glass. The aroma of basil and the touch of sweetness from the cucumber juice create a fresh and light experience.

Ingredients:
6 cl cucumber juice (leave the peels)
1.5 cl fresh lime juice
1,5 cl agave nectar
5 basil leaves

Preparation:

Mix the basil leaves in a baking dish.
Add the other ingredients. Shake with ice.
Strain through a tea strainer with fresh ice.
Peel the cucumber. Garnish with cucumber ribbons.

CHERRY LIME SPRITZ

This festive and sparkling Cherry Lime Spritzer offers a tart touch. You can sweeten it with a simple syrup or stevia drops naturally without using sugar for a low carb option.

Ingredients:

2 lime wedges
2 tbsp. freshly squeezed lime juice
2 tbsp. 100% cherry juice
2 tbsp. simple syrup (or 4 drops of liquid stevia, or to taste)
3/4 cup of your favorite sparkling water
additional lime wedges for garnish (optional)

Preparation:

Put 2 lime wedges in the bottom of the glass. Destroy the wedges with a jumbled tool.
Add lime juice, cherry juice, and sweetener of your choice and mix up more.
Pour carbonated water into the glass.
Add a few ice cubes. Garnish with additional lime wedges if desired.

CRANBERRY MOCKTAIL 2

This sparkling sweet mocktail is not only good for the palate but also good for the gut. Kombucha gives this mocktail some fizz, while a blend of pomegranate and orange juice blends sour with sweet.

Ingredients:
1 cup of crushed ice
1 cup cranberry kombucha *
1/2 cup of pomegranate juice
1/2 cup of freshly squeezed orange juice

Preparation:
Pour all the ingredients into a serving glass and mix until well blended.

* Kombucha is not technically alcohol-free, as the fermentation process creates a very small amount of alcohol. If you prefer a 100% soft drink, replace the kombucha with ginger beer or another flavored soda.

MINT MATCHA CHILLER

Our mocktail list couldn't be complete without some matcha. This minty take on the popular drink will leave you energized and refreshed.

Ingredients:

12 cl chilled sparkling water
4–5 mint leaves, chopped
1 teaspoon of lemon juice
1 teaspoon of matcha green tea powder

Preparation:

Pour all the ingredients into a serving glass. Mix until combined.

COLD COFFEE MOCKTAIL

If you are looking for that classic blend of cream and coffee, this is your drink.

Ingredients:

3/4 cup of coconut cream
3/4 cup of cold coffee
4 tsp birch xylitol
1/2 tsp. almond extract
1 tablespoon. raw cocoa powder
unsweetened chocolate flakes and coconut whipped cream for garnish

Preparation:

Pour all the ingredients into a serving glass. Blend until combined.
Top with unsweetened chocolate chips and coconut whipped cream.

MOCKTAIL CHAI

This tasty drink offers a fun chai twist with the health benefits of turmeric. Featuring sweet almonds and Ceylon tea, this blend has a slightly sweet side with a hint of caffeine.

Ingredients:

1/2 cup of turmeric almond juice
1/2 cup of Ceylon tea
1/2 tsp. almond extract
3/4 cup cream or coconut cream
cinnamon stick

Preparation:

Pour all the ingredients into a serving glass.
Mix until combined.
Garnish with a cinnamon stick.

LEMON WITH COCONUT

This cooling combination of coconut water, lime and rosemary blends different flavors for a sweet and tart taste. Meanwhile, rosemary adds flavor to your glass.

Ingredients:

1/2 cup of coconut water
1/2 cup of tonic water, chilled
1 tablespoon. lime juice
pinch of rosemary for garnish
lime zest for garnish

Preparation:

Pour all the ingredients into a serving glass. Mix until combined.
Garnish with spiral lime, rosemary and lime zest.

POMEGRANATE TWIST

If you're looking for a Christmas drink that looks and tastes like the New Year, try this pomegranate twist mocktail. As an added bonus, it contains ingredients you may already have in your kitchen.

Ingredients:

1/2 cup of sparkling water
1/4 cup pomegranate juice com
ice
orange zest for garnish

Preparation:

In a glass, add ice and pour all the ingredients.
Mix and garnish with a fresh orange twist.

MINT WATERMELON

Do you miss summer so much? Dive into this mocktail to satisfy your craving for one of the most hydrating fruits of the summer.

Ingredients:

1/2 cup cold pressed watermelon juice
1 tablespoon. freshly squeezed lime
2 mint leaves

fresh mint for garnish
lime zest for garnish

Preparation:

Pour all the ingredients into a shaker with a handful of ice. Shake for 30 seconds to 1 minute.
Garnish with fresh mint and lime zest.
Serve on ice.

CARROTS GINGER BOOCH

Looking for a mocktail that will help you get more beta-carotene in your diet? This crisp, bright mocktail is great for those who love ginger, lemon, and the slight sweetness of carrot juice.

Ingredients:

1/2 cup cold pressed carrot juice
1/2 cup ginger and lemon kombucha.
1 tablespoon. fresh lemon juice

Preparation:

Pour all the ingredients into a serving glass.
Mix until combined.
Have fun right away.

CRAN-STRAWBERRY

Do you like strawberries and the tartness of cranberries? Try this bubbly kombucha tail with a splash of cranberry juice and sparkling water.

Ingredients:

1/2 cup strawberry flavored sparkling water
1/4 cup of organic cranberry juice
1/2 cup of Health-Ade's original kombucha
freshly cut strawberries for garnish

Preparation:

Pour all the ingredients into a serving glass.
Stir until everything is well blended.
Garnish with sliced strawberries.

THE TART OG

This mocktail is perfect if you want something tart and fresh that will give you an extra thirst-quenching touch to your evening or afternoon.

Ingredients;

1 cup of sparkling water
Juice of 1 lime
juice of 1 lemon
fresh mint for garnish

Preparation:

Pour all the ingredients into a serving glass. Stir until everything is well blended.

INFUSION OF ROSE

If you are one of the floral drink lovers, this light and sweet drink is perfect for you.

Ingredients:

1/2 cup of rose tea infusion
1/2 cup of berry sparkling water

1 tablespoon. fresh lemon juice
1-2 drops of stevia, optional

Preparation:

Pour all the ingredients into a serving glass. Stir until everything is blended.

THREE MOCKTAILS BASED ON TEA

1) Green tea, ginger and pineapple mocktail

Ingredients:

6 mint leaves
1 tablespoon of ginger juice
½ tablespoon of lime juice
50 ml of sugar syrup
30ml cold Matcha green tea, mint and licorice
½ slice of fresh pineapple in cubes
1 slice of lime
to taste candied ginger
1 sprig of mint

Preparation:

Mash the pineapple in the shaker and then add all the other ingredients. Shake for a few seconds and pour your mocktail through a colander into a glass with some ice cubes. Decorate with a slice of lime, candied ginger and a sprig of mint.

2) Peach and rosemary iced tea

Ingredients for the syrup:

1 dl of water
75 g of sugar
200 g of diced peaches
Ingredients for the mocktail:

¾ of liter of water
1 Earl Gray Everton tea bag
3 sprigs of rosemary
½ lemon
½ peach in wedges

Preparation:

Boil the water with the sugar in a saucepan. Add the peaches and cook for about 10 minutes. Now, remove from the heat and let the syrup flavor for about an hour.

Meanwhile, boil the tea water and let our Earl Gray with rosemary infuse for about 15 minutes. Remove the sachets and the rosemary and add the peach syrup and the juice of ½ lemon. Let it cool and put everything in the refrigerator for about 1 hour. Serve it to your guests with peach wedges, rosemary and ice cubes.

3) Raspberry Splash

Ingredients:

4 dl of water
2 Earl Gray Everton tea bags
½ file
3 dl of ginger ale
8 sprigs of mint
80 g of raspberries
to taste ice cubes
Preparation:

Bring the water to a boil and add the Earl Gray sachets, leaving to infuse for about 5 minutes. Squeeze the lime and mix the juice with the cooled black tea and ginger ale. Spread the mint, raspberries and ice cubes in 4 glasses. Pour in the tea and voila… your mocktail is ready to serve.

10 MOCKTAILS IDEAS SUITABLE FOR EVERY NEED

Sweet Adeline Warm Drink

It's sweet, it's innocent, and it's the perfect hot drink for a cold winter night. Warm and comfortable, this sweet recipe from Adeline is a good way to spice up your tea routine. It is the perfect drink for cold days and the sweet, slightly spicy flavor is a pure delight.

The recipe is incredibly simple and it all starts with fresh pomegranate juice and a homemade cinnamon syrup. You will also need black tea with a blend of spiced orange and hot water. Finish it with a cinnamon stick and get ready to be won over by its flavor.

Mocktail Mojito Holiday Pomegranate

Mojito is a great drink, but it doesn't have to be relegated to summer or necessarily include rum. This variation is seasonally perfect and alcohol-free, making it the ideal mix for the whole family.

To do this, you will need fresh mint, lime, pomegranate juice and lemonade. It's topped with a light soda to give it a nice sparkle. Since pomegranates are in season, be sure to include seeds for the perfect finishing touch.

Baby Bellini Non alcoholic cocktail

Bellini is another fantastic drink that many of us enjoy for brunch. It adds a great fruity smoothie to your day and is incredibly easy to turn into a non-alcoholic delight.

The little Bellini is just as simple to prepare and just as pleasant to the taste of the original. Peach nectar and sparkling cider are the only ingredients you need, and there are no special tools or techniques involved. Just pour in and have fun finding the doses and variations you like best.

Hot Not Toddy

Make a relaxing, warm drink with your favorite tea. The recipe is simple and can be customized with various teas and sweeteners.

The basic recipe sweetens hot tea with honey and adds acidity with a little lemon to give it an invigorating touch. Add spices such as cinnamon, cloves and nutmeg and for a more inviting and comforting drink.

Virgin Mary Cocktail

There is something about a cold winter morning that brings out the desire for a Bloody Mary. It's a great drink for watching a good movie or just relaxing before the day begins. Still, there's no need to pour the vodka.

Virgin Mary is a healthy and invigorating drink and won't make you miss the alcohol. The spicy tomato juice mix includes Worcestershire and spicy sauces, pepper, celery salt and a squeeze of lemon. Garnish with a pickle or celery, or both.

Sparkling Peach Sunrise

If you're in the mood for a very fruity drink, this is the recipe for you. It has an excellent fruit flavor, a hint of sweetness and is very refreshing.

Inspired by the famous tequila sunrise, the sparkling peach sunrise eliminates the distillate and replaces it with peach juice combined with orange juice. Grenadine remains the fruity sweetener that gives it its characteristic sunrise effect. Top it all off with your favorite citrus soda and a delicious mocktail is ready for you to enjoy.

Sparkling Mocktail Sundowner

An ideal drink for your summer sunset dinners. On vacation this cocktail is a sparkling and refreshing pleasure to drink that you can pour into a glass or prepare in a pitcher to share with your friends, in both cases it is a very simple and quick recipe to prepare.

The recipe calls for white grape juice, rather than the purple variety, which is relatively easier to find on the market. The only other ingredients are sparkling water and fresh mint. The trio of ingredients creates a drink that pairs perfectly with any food on your table.

El Submarino

A different way to enjoy hot chocolate, el submarino is a pleasure for the whole family. This recipe comes from Argentina and can delight children anywhere in the world.

Instead of making the classic hot chocolate, you will heat the milk and sweeten it with sugar and vanilla. You will also need a quality chocolate bar, which will be dipped into the steaming cup and slowly melt. It's a pretty fun variation that will give your winter a unique twist.

Non alcoholic eggnog

There are many eggnog recipes available but by eliminating the liquor you can create a family-friendly version. So, if you are looking for a genuine non-alcoholic recipe, this is an excellent choice.

This eggnog also eliminates the fear of drinking raw eggs, so it's even safer for the whole family. The eggs are lightly cooked with sugar and salt before adding the milk. It's not the fastest way to get eggnog, but it's certainly the most reliable.

Hong Kong milk tea

For a truly unique drink, make a cup of Hong Kong milk tea during the holiday season. This is a succulent, creamy cup of tea that you won't want to miss.

The recipe only requires three ingredients. Heat the water and choose your favorite black tea. Add evaporated milk or, to make it a little sweeter, condensed milk or sugar according to your taste. This mocktail is easy to make and can be served hot or cold, depending on your mood.

MOCKTAIL SPRITZ

The recipe for this cool alcohol-free cocktail to drink in company with friends:

INGREDIENTS for 4 people:
ORANGE JUICE 500ml
BITTER 250ml
TONIC WATER 100ml
ICE to taste
ORANGE 4 slices

• 34 kcal The calories refer to 100 g of product

The non-alcoholic spritz is a variant of the most famous Italian aperitif ever. In every respectable aperitif or happy hour break, the spritz cannot be missing, accompanied by snacks or delicious preparations, now cheers the afternoons and palates of Italians. The spritz is an alcoholic aperitif based on prosecco, bitters and Seltz but also those who prefer to enjoy an aperitif with friends without drinking alcohol can still enjoy this cocktail in its non-alcoholic variant based on fresh orange juice.

How to prepare the non-alcoholic spritz:

Take a glass with a wide base or if you prefer a large wine glass and fill it with 4/5 ice cubes. You can help yourself with a cocktail measuring cup or imagine that your glass is divided into parts: then pour in sequence two parts of orange juice, one part of non-alcoholic bitter and one part of tonic water (3). Mix everything with a spoon turning from bottom to top, garnish with a slice of orange and enjoy this very fresh non-alcoholic aperitif.

Variants
Spritz with pomegranate
For an even tastier and more fruity aperitif, combine your ingredients with pomegranate seeds blended in a mixer and brown sugar, in this variant use less orange juice.

Spritz history

That of Spritz is a rather ancient and curious story. This sweet-tasting aperitif with a rather low alcohol content has its roots between the end of the 18th and the beginning of the 19th century in the areas of Lombardy-Veneto dominated at that time by the Austrian government. It is said that the Hapsburg armies considered Venetian wines "too strong" and that for this reason they used sparkling water. Hence the origin of the name from the German verb "spritzen" which means "to spray". Over time the sparkling water was replaced by Seltz water and only in the 1920s was bitter added to the original recipe. Today prosecco is preferred to white wine to which Campari Spritz and Aperol Spritz are added in its most famous variations,

WATER BASED MOCKTAILS.

Flavored water: benefits and recipes

Flavored water is a drink that helps hydrate and purify with taste, providing the body with vitamins, minerals and antioxidant molecules

Flavored water is a non-alcoholic vitamin drink also known as detox water, which helps you hydrate and purify with taste.

Free of calories, good to drink and colorful, it is in effect a cold maceration, which is prepared by adding completely natural ingredients such as fresh fruit, vegetables, herbs and spices to the water. These ingredients transfer beneficial substances to the water and give it unique and very pleasant flavors. The result is flavored water: a good, refreshing and healthy drink, which can be consumed by adults and children without limits, also perfect for those on a diet.

The main benefits of flavored water are to improve the daily water intake and to provide the body with precious minerals, vitamins and substances with an antioxidant action.

What are the benefits?
We all know how important it is to drink at least one and a half liters of water a day to keep our body healthy. When we drink more water, we can immediately appreciate the benefits on the mind and body, even on an aesthetic level.

A greater supply of water, in addition to making us feel more energetic and more concentrated, makes the skin softer and firmer, visibly improves the complexion of the epidermis and ensures that water retention and cellulite are significantly reduced. This happens because water is the most abundant element in our organism and represents a fundamental component of the intracellular and extracellular environments, the latter consisting of plasma, lymph, interstitial fluid and liquor, or cephalorachidian fluid. Inside our body, water acts as a solvent for inorganic ions, sugars, amino acids, proteins and other molecules and allows the absorption and transport of nutrients and the removal and excretion of waste substances.

However, many people struggle to cover their daily water needs and, in this case, flavored water can be of great help. In fact, thanks to the pleasant taste and appearance of the flavored water, you are more inclined to drink, thus ensuring the right amount of water. In addition, the maceration of fruit, vegetables, aromatic herbs and spices transfers a good amount of beneficial substances for the body to the water including mineral salts, water-soluble vitamins and flavonoids, molecules with a powerful antioxidant action useful for counteracting the damage caused by radicals. free.

How to prepare flavored water
Preparing flavored water is really simple, fast and affordable for everyone. Just get a glass jug and strainer or a container for infusion, seasonal fruit and vegetables, fresh or dried herbs and spices. The fruits most used in the preparation of flavored water or detox water are citrus fruits, kiwi, peaches, grapes, pineapple and red fruits,

while among vegetables cucumbers, fennel and celery are often used.

The process to obtain the flavored water then takes a few minutes: after washing and coarsely cutting the fruit and vegetables, they are placed in the jug, add aromatic herbs and spices to taste and cover with mineral or filtered water, smooth. or even carbonated.

The water is then left to macerate for twelve to twenty-four hours, preferably at room temperature and placing a lid on the jug. At the end of maceration, it is filtered and poured into a bottle or flask to take with you outside the home.

The flavored water can be kept in the refrigerator or at room temperature and can be consumed without limits throughout the day, even with meals: it does not provide calories, hydrates and refreshes and is suitable for all ages without any contraindications.

Better recipes

Here are some recipes to prepare flavored water for every need. The procedure is the same for each recipe: in a carafe, washed and cut fruit and vegetables, spices and aromatic herbs are placed and covered with two liters of water.

Draining flavored water

Helps drain excess fluids and counter swelling, water retention and cellulite.

a cucumber cut into slices
half fennel cut into slices
a stick of celery cut into rings
a handful of sage leaves

Digestive flavored water

To be sipped to counter abdominal bloating, slow digestion and a sense of heaviness.

an apple cut into slices
four or five cardamom seeds
a teaspoon of fennel seeds
one centimeter of ginger root

Antioxidant flavored water

Useful for filling up with antioxidant molecules, useful for counteracting the damage caused by free radicals.

five or six strawberries cut in half
two tablespoons of blackberries
a spoonful of raspberries
a spoonful of pomegranate grains
a slice of lemon
two sprigs of rosemary

Refreshing flavored water

Perfect in summer, to hydrate and quench your thirst with taste.

five slices of diced pineapple
three slices of lime
a handful of mint leaves
Warming flavored water
Excellent to be enjoyed on cold winter days for its tonic and warming action.

two sliced apples
five or six cinnamon sticks

With imagination and creativity, many other recipes can be created and always different flavored waters can be prepared.

SMOOTHIES

A smoothie is a mixed and sometimes sweetened drink made from fresh fruit and in special cases it may contain chocolate or peanut butter. In addition to fruit, many smoothies include crushed ice, frozen fruit, honey, or contain syrups and frozen ingredients. They have a very thick and creamy texture, which is a specific feature of these drinks. They can also contain milk, yogurt or ice cream. Smoothies are often marketed to people who care about their health and for this reason some restaurants offer ingredients such as soy milk, whey powder, green tea, herbal supplements or nutritional supplements; in fact, smoothies are an excellent idea for a fresh and thirst-quenching break, but also to enjoy all the goodness of fruit and vegetables and to better preserve the organoleptic properties and the benefits of the ingredients we use, but above all, with vegetables and fruit in season they are delicious and already sweet at the right point, so much so that they do not require the addition of additional sugars. They are also an excellent idea as a quick dessert to offer your children for a snack to convince them to eat a little more fruit in the summer.

The electric blender started the smoothie trend in the United States. The word "smoothie" was first consecrated by Mabel Stegner on June 23, 1940 in an article entitled "Let the blender do it for you!" Published by the New York Herald Tribune. Regarding the ingredients, he wrote: "For example, put a few ounces of milk, fruit juice, tomato juice or any desired liquid in the food container."

So the term "smoothie" means creamy, velvety and has its origins in the 40s on the West Coast of the United States, where recipes with simply blended fruit and vegetables were in vogue, then over the years ingredients such as ice or the milk.

With the 1960s the popularity of smoothies became ever greater, especially among vegetarians, macrobiotics and vegans who used the mixer a lot to blend their foods, not only fruit, but also vegetables.

Smoothies were a very popular drink even among the hippies of the seventies, and so on every decade has seen smoothies protagonists in the USA as a trend of the most disparate groups, including sports and fitness lovers.

Today the smoothie is a very popular drink both in the United States and in the rest of the world, where themed "Smoothie bars" are proliferating, where everything has gone through the blender and the smoothie method is also used to make cocktails.

Middle Eastern cuisine also makes extensive use of smoothies, think for example of the Indian sharbat, a smoothie made with yogurt, honey and fresh fruit, or the tota puri mango, a smoothie made with mango, ice and brown sugar.

Unlike smoothies, smoothies do not contain sugar or milk and are ice-free.

They are not even centrifuged, which are the pure extraction of fruit and vegetable juices, they do not contain ice cream like milkshakes but are low in calories and are often made with water or sometimes with the addition of yogurt, or a few tablespoons of vegetable milk obviously for those who follow a vegan diet, it is advisable to ask if you are in some trendy place always soy yogurt.

6 FRUIT SMOOTHIES

1 Strawberry and coconut smoothie

200 g Strawberries
120 ml Coconut Milk
2 teaspoons Honey
2 ice cubes

2 Apricot and peach smoothie

100 g Apricots
100 g Nectarines
2 drops Vanilla Extract
120 ml Rice Milk
2 teaspoons Agave Syrup
2 ice cubes

3 Banana and cinnamon smoothie

200 g Bananas
120 ml Almond Milk
1 pinch Cinnamon powder
2 teaspoons Honey
2 ice cubes

4 Fig and ginger smoothie

200 g Figs
120 ml Coconut Milk
1 pinch Ginger powder
2 teaspoons Honey
3 teaspoons Chocolate Codette
2 ice cubes

Raspberry and almond smoothie

250 g Fresh Raspberries (then frozen)
100 ml Almond Milk
2 tablespoons Brown Sugar
3 teaspoons Sugar Colored sprinkles

6 Blueberry Smoothie

250 g Fresh blueberries (then frozen)
100 ml Coconut Milk
2 teaspoons Brown Sugar

Preparation Valid for all Smoothies

To prepare the recipe for fruit smoothies, wash and chop the fruits of the smoothie you have chosen to make, remove the peel (if you want).

Put the fruit, honey or sugar in the blender depending on the recipe and the milk, operate and in a few minutes you will have a fresh and tasty nectar to quench your thirst and integrate your diet with vitamins and minerals.

We advise you to taste the smoothie before pouring it in order to add fruit, sugar or liquids, depending on your taste.

After pouring into glasses decorated with sprinkles of sugar or chocolate or a pinch of cinnamon depending on the recipe and serve.

After pouring into glasses decorated with sprinkles of sugar or chocolate or a pinch of cinnamon depending on the recipe and serve.

8 SMOOTHIES RECIPES A MUST TRY

Smoothie with apple and cinnamon

The apple and cinnamon smoothie recipe is very light, as it provides very few kilocalories. It is recommended for everyone, for a quick and healthy snack, and especially for those who want to keep fit. This smoothie is an ideal recipe to prepare in autumn or winter and can be enjoyed by people with celiac disease, as it is gluten-free, and also by those who have eliminated all animal derivatives from their diet. For the preparation we will use vegetable milk, so even lactose intolerant can consume this smoothie.

Preparation:

10 min Calories / portion: 110 kcal

Portion: about 250 ml Ingredients (Serves 2): 2 Apples (about 300 gr without core and peel) 1 tablespoon of lemon juice 200 ml of millet milk 1 teaspoon of cinnamon

Method:
First wash the apples, peel them and remove the core; Cut the apples into small pieces and place them in the blender with the millet milk and lemon juice, which serves to prevent the apple from turning black; Operate the blender until you get a foam and finally add the cinnamon powder; Pour into 2 glasses and enjoy with a straw.

Storage and advice: the apple and cinnamon smoothie must be consumed immediately, so as not to lose the beneficial properties of the apple. For those who want to prepare an even lighter smoothie, you can replace millet milk with low-mineral water. If you want a sweeter flavor, you can sweeten with a teaspoon of stevia-based sweetener powder.

Smoothie with avocado, spinach, banana and chia seeds

The smoothie with avocado, spinach, banana and chia seeds is an ideal recipe for those suffering from fatigue and feeling down, so we recommend it whenever you need to recharge and recharge your batteries. It is also suitable for celiacs, as there is the total absence of gluten. The smoothie can be consumed by both vegans and vegetarians, as it is free of ingredients of animal origin. Finally, it is lactose-free, so even those who are intolerant to this sugar can drink it.

Preparation:

15 min Calories / portion: 190 kcal

Portion: about 250 ml Ingredients (Serves 2): 1 Ripe Avocado (about 100 grams, without peel and seed) 1 Ripe Banana (about 100 grams, without peel) 50 grams of Spinach 1 tablespoon of Chia seeds 1 tablespoon of Lemon juice 100 ml of Rice milk

Method:

Prepare all the ingredients: wash the spinach and drain well; wash the avocado, peel it, remove the internal seed and cut it into small pieces; peel the banana and cut it into small pieces. Pour the spinach, avocado and banana pieces into the blender, then add the lemon juice, chia seeds and rice milk. Check the result and add more rice milk if the smoothie seems too solid, then blend again for a few seconds. Pour the smoothie into two glasses or 2 glass bottles and garnish with two straws.

Storage and advice: the smoothie should be consumed immediately after preparation to preserve vitamins and antioxidants as much as possible. Otherwise, you can keep it in the fridge for a couple of hours at the most. Rice milk can be substituted for another plant-based milk, such as millet milk or soy milk. To further flavor the smoothie, we can add a tablespoon of unsweetened cocoa powder. Make sure the avocado is fully ripe to make the smoothie, otherwise it can be bitter. To check it, you just need to press a finger on the peel, if it is ripe it will be soft.

Pumpkin smoothie with oat flakes, cinnamon and star anise

This smoothie is based on pumpkin, so it is ideal to prepare in the fall, when this vegetable is in season, providing us with all the nutrients we need to face the winter. Pumpkin is in fact rich in beta-carotene, a precious antioxidant, fiber and mineral salts such as magnesium, useful for the nervous system, and potassium, which counteracts water retention. We have embellished the pumpkin smoothie with cinnamon which boasts, among others, antibacterial and anti-inflammatory properties, star anise, diuretic and antibacterial, and ground oat flakes, which give the smoothie satiating and reducing properties against the cholesterol present. in the blood. Let's see what we need for this recipe and what procedure to follow.

Preparation:

15 min Calories / serving: 197 kcal

Portion: about 250 ml Ingredients (Doses for 1 person): 200 gr of clean pumpkin (already peeled and seeded) 1 large orange 20 gr of oat flakes A pinch of ground cinnamon A pinch of star anise powder Cinnamon stick (to decorate) Star anise (to decorate)

Method:

First, place the oat flakes in a hot pan and toast them for 5 minutes, turning them constantly so as not to burn them. In the meantime that the oat flakes cool, dry the pumpkin and cut it into pieces of about 2 cm. When cold, chop the rolled oats in a blender and set aside. Put the pumpkin, the juice of one orange, a pinch of ground cinnamon and one of star anise powder in the blender and blend until smooth. If necessary, add water until you get the desired consistency. Pour the mixture into a glass and garnish with the chopped oat flakes, a cinnamon stick and a piece of star anise. Storage and tips Like all smoothies, this one should be consumed immediately after preparation. Alternatively, you can store it in the fridge for up to two or three hours. Instead of orange juice, you can use lemon juice for a greater purifying and detoxifying effect. If it turns out to be bitter, you can sweeten the smoothie with a teaspoon of honey or a stevia-based sweetener.

Chocolate smoothie with chia seeds and banana

The chocolate smoothie with chia seeds and banana is a perfect recipe to break the mid-morning or afternoon hunger, without falling into less healthy temptations such as snacks or snacks. To prepare a good homemade smoothie, a blender and simple and carefully chosen ingredients are enough: in this case, the shopping basket contains mainly bananas, dates, bitter cocoa, dark chocolate, almond milk, chia seeds and grated coconut . Due to its ingredients, in particular dates, coconut and dark chocolate, it is a rather caloric smoothie, ideal for regaining energy in the middle of the morning but to be consumed in moderation, especially for those on a diet or otherwise attentive to the figure.

Preparation:

10 min Calories / portion: 440 kcal

Portion: about 250/300 ml Ingredients (Doses for 1 person): 1 Banana 2 tablespoons of bitter cocoa 5 Dates 3 ice cubes (optional) 30 g of extra dark chocolate 1 tablespoon of chia seeds 1 tablespoon of grated coconut 140 ml of Almond milk

Method:

First, peel the banana, cut it into chunks and remove the stones from the dates. Put the bananas and dates inside the blender along with the ice (optional), the coconut, the bitter cocoa and the almond milk. Operate the blender until you get a velvety, smooth and homogeneous smoothie. Serve the smoothie in a glass and garnish with extra dark chocolate flakes and chia seeds. If you want an "eat and drink" smoothie, add a few slices of banana.

Storage and advice: If you do not want to consume it immediately, you can put the smoothie in the fridge and consume it, if possible, within a couple of hours. If you don't like almond milk, you can replace it with oat or soy milk, depending on your taste. In addition, we recommend using fairly ripe bananas, which are sweeter and better suited to the recipe.

Blueberry smoothie with oat milk and banana

Among the long line of colorful smoothies, one of our favorites is certainly the banana smoothie with blueberries and oat milk. The sweetness and body of banana mix with the woody flavor of blueberries to create a refreshing and sweet drink. The oat milk with a neutral flavor and high nutritional properties helps the smoothie to achieve the creaminess that distinguishes it. So let's find out how to prepare a perfect blueberry smoothie with oat milk and banana at home. As with all smoothies, the quality of the fruit is of paramount importance. Good fruit = good smoothie.

The equation is as easy as the process of this fresh and cheerful recipe.

Preparation:

5 min Calories / serving: 164 kcal

Serving size: about 200 ml Ingredients (Serves 2): 2 bananas 250 g of blueberries 4 ice cubes (optional) 250 ml oat milk

Method:

First, wash the blueberries carefully. Peel the banana and cut it into small pieces. Put the fruit, ice and half of the almond milk in the special container and turn on the blender. Add water or other oat milk to taste, until you reach the consistency you want for your smoothie. Serve the blueberry smoothie with oat milk and banana in a glass, garnish it with banana and fresh blueberries, if necessary.

Storage and advice: Also in this case it is advisable to drink the smoothie within a couple of hours so as not to lose its nutritional properties. If you don't like oat milk, you can replace it with almond or soy milk. For the preparation of smoothies and smoothies, we recommend using fairly ripe bananas, which are sweeter and better suited to this type of preparation.

Peach smoothie with almond milk and fresh mint

We now offer you a quick and easy recipe to prepare a peach-based summer smoothie with almond milk and fresh mint. The sweetness of peaches and almond milk is combined with the slight acidity of yogurt and the freshness of mint creating an irresistible mix with exotic references. And in case the straw isn't for you, pour the smoothie into a bowl, enrich it with a little fresh peach cut into cubes, some rolled oats and enjoy it in spoonfuls.

Preparation:

10 min Calories / portion: 190 kcal

Portion: about 200 ml Ingredients (Serves 2): 2 ripe peaches 150 ml of almond milk

80 g of white soy yogurt 6 leaves of fresh mint 3 ice cubes

Method:

Wash the peaches thoroughly under running water. Peel and remove the core. Then cut them roughly into pieces. Clean the mint leaves with a wet sponge. Pour the chopped peaches, almond milk, white yogurt, ice and 4 mint leaves into the blender. Operate the blender and leave it on until you have obtained a smooth and full-bodied smoothie. Serve the smoothie in a glass with a decorative mint leaf.

Storage and advice: We recommend drinking this freshly made smoothie, given the use of perishable foods. If you don't like soy yogurt you can replace it with lean cow's milk or with a vegetable drink of your choice, to be added until the desired consistency is obtained.

Antioxidant smoothie with watermelon and grapes

The antioxidant smoothie with watermelon and grapes is an ideal drink to prepare and consume in the summer when these fruits are in season, to fully benefit from their nutritional properties. The presence of watermelon and grapes gives the smoothie many properties: benefits for the visual function and for the pain of arthritis, anti-aging action, diuretic effect, lowering of pressure and prevention of cardiovascular diseases. As always, we advise you to use fruit from organic farming, without pesticides and harmful substances.

Preparation:
15 min Calories / portion: 165 kcal

Portion: about 200 ml Ingredients (Serves 2): 250 gr of watermelon (weight without peel) 200 gr of black grapes, with or without seeds 2 tablespoons of fresh lime juice

Method:

Slice the watermelon and put it in the blender, then wash the grapes and cut the berries in half, also removing the seeds. Add the grapes to the blender along with the lime juice and a pinch of salt and blend for at least 30 seconds, until you have a creamy consistency. 3If it is too dry, add a few more drops of lime juice.

Storage and Tips: Drink this freshly made smoothie to benefit from all the nutrients, but slowly to aid digestion. If you don't have lime, you can replace it with lemon.

Frozen smoothies with ginger and peanut butter

We want to conclude this series of smoothie recipes with an iced version, to be enjoyed in the summer instead of the classic popsicle. Refreshing, energetic and nourishing, with a light digestive action, in fact, this frozen smoothie is ideal for a healthy snack or for a fresh and healthy snack with all the beneficial properties of ginger. As always, we advise you to use fruit from organic farming, without pesticides and harmful substances. Now let's see how to make these ginger frozen smoothies at home.

Ingredients (Serves 2):

3 Ripe bananas 1 piece of fresh ginger root (about 4/5 cm) 75 ml of unsweetened almond milk 1 tablespoon of agave syrup 1 tablespoon of lemon juice 2 teaspoons of organic peanut butter

Method:

For this recipe choose fairly ripe and soft bananas. Peel the bananas, cut them into small pieces and sprinkle them with lemon juice to prevent them from blackening. Peel the ginger and cut into thin slices, then transfer all the ingredients to the blender glass and operate intermittently until a soft and creamy consistency is obtained. Wet a popsicle mold and pour in the smoothie, insert some toothpicks. Place the mold in the freezer for 6/7 hours, preferably overnight, to allow the smoothies to solidify. Before using them, immerse the mold for a few seconds in warm water to extract the frozen smoothies more easily.

Storage and tips: Unlike other smoothies, you can consume this when you like it. In fact, storage in the freezer guarantees a long life. If you love the flavor of this smoothie and want to enjoy it outside the summer season, omit the freezing phase, you will have a soft smoothie suitable for all months of the year.

MORE 15 IDEAS TO MAKE GREAT SMOOTHIES

1. Mango smoothie

The mango smoothie is very simple, but its summery scent will know how to win you over. Blend 500 g of low-fat white yogurt, 250 g of peeled mango cut into small pieces and a couple of teaspoons of brown sugar to taste for 1 minute.

2. Energizing smoothie

Energy discharges? Don't worry, here's the energizing smoothie recipe! Put in the blender 1 pear, peeled and cut into pieces, a handful of skinless and roughly chopped almonds, 1 low-fat white yogurt and a few tablespoons of coconut milk. Blend all the ingredients for 1 minute and serve with ice cubes to taste.

3. Kiwi smoothie

Simple but truly delicious, the kiwi smoothie is made in seconds and is perfect for serving at Sunday brunch. Blend 1 kiwi, a few tablespoons of plain water, 2 teaspoons of brown sugar and a glass of kiwi juice for about a minute.

4. Refreshing smoothie

For all the summer days when the heat will take away your concentration and energy, the refreshing smoothie will be a real elixir of well-being. Blend 1 lemon, 2 pears (replaceable with apples or bananas), 2 peaches and a handful of watercress.

5. Exotic smoothie

The exotic smoothie will bring a touch of joy and summer to your snacks. Prepare it by blending 3 bananas, 1 mango and a nice glass of blood orange juice. Put the smoothie in a jug and add ice cubes to taste.

6. Detoxifying smoothie

Did you overdo it with dinner last night? Do you come out of a period in which you always had lunch out? The only solution to get yourself back on track is a nice detox diet in which to introduce this special detoxifying smoothie. Blend 200 ml of coconut milk, a handful of rocket and a pinch of pepper or nutmeg.

7. Anti-stress smoothie

To combat stress, there is an effective and tasty smoothie recipe. Blend a handful of kale, a few leaves of fresh mint, 1 orange and 1 lemon, you will overcome stress and your palate will thank you!

8. Regenerating red fruit smoothie

When you feel a little undertone, you can choose to stay indoors or, alternatively, to prepare yourself a delicious rejuvenating red fruit smoothie that will get you back on track. Blend a handful of dried Goji berries, a handful of blackberries, a stick of celery crushed with a potato peeler and cut into pieces and a few lettuce leaves.

9. Stimulating smoothie

This smoothie will also be perfect to make you recover from lack of energy due to too much fatigue, but not only that: it will also make you recover your good mood in a very short time. Blend 1 peeled cucumber, 1 avocado, 5 radishes and 1 lemon.

10. Vitamin smoothie

The recipe for this smoothie is a real ultra-vitamin concentrate that will be good for your whole body. Blend 2 blood oranges, a generous handful of blueberries and 2 tablespoons of blackberries for one minute. Delicious and thirst-quenching.

11. Spring smoothie

A smoothie for every season: for spring, when the first heat begins to feel, you can opt for something fresh and tasty. Mint is the perfect ingredient for a drink with these two characteristics.

Cucumber is another product to use, to then combine the flavors with a little lemon and, for those who like it, some ice to make this smoothie even more refreshing.

12. Summer smoothie

For the summer, the desire for fruit is even greater: a strawberry and watermelon smoothie is ideal for cooling down but also for receiving vitamins and nutrients so as to give strength to the body during the heat.

To prepare it, use a greater amount of watermelon than the strawberry in the blender: you can then decorate the glass with pieces of strawberry on top to taste.

13. Spinach smoothie

Yes, even spinach can be used to prepare one of the most particular smoothies. To do this, add this vegetable to a blender with a banana and two apples: the fruit will thus give a sweet and easier to drink flavor to the drink.

14. Smoothie with carrots

Another smoothie with strong flavors but invigorating and healthy for the body is the one with carrots, which have the power to facilitate the tan. Also in this case, use the banana as a base for the smoothie and add the pineapple in the blender to give consistency and add a not too intense flavor to that of the carrots.

15. Digestive smoothie

Smoothies are a fairly light type of drink, since thanks to the presence of fruits and vegetables they do not weigh too much on the stomach and digestion. Indeed they can be used for this: a smoothie made with bananas, pineapple, lemon and ginger promotes digestion.

10 DAYS 10 SLIMMING SMOOTHIES

1st day
Green vegetables and mixed fruits

• 3 handfuls of spinach • 2 cups of water • 1 apple without core • 1 cup of mango peeled and chopped into pieces • 1 cup of strawberries • 1 handful of seedless grapes • 1 sachet of stevia based sweetener (add more if necessary) • 2 tablespoons of flaxseed powder
Optional: 1 scoop of protein powder
Blend the spinach in the water until you get a green juice. Add the remaining ingredients and continue until the mixture has a creamy consistency.

II Day
Apple and strawberry

• 3 handfuls of mixed salad • 2 cups of water • 1 banana • 2 peeled and cored apples • ½ cup of strawberries • 2 sachets of stevia based sweetener (add more if necessary) • 2 tablespoons of flaxseed powder

Optional: 1 scoop of protein powder
Blend the mixed salad in the water until you get a green juice. Add the remaining ingredients and continue until the mixture has a creamy consistency.

III Day
Apple and blueberry

• 1 handful of mixed salad • 1 handful of spinach • 2 cups of water • ½ cup of blueberries • 1 banana • 1 peeled and cored apple • 1 sachet of stevia based sweetener • 2 tablespoons of flaxseed powder
Optional: 1 scoop of protein powder
Blend the mixed salad and spinach in the water until you get a green juice. Add the remaining ingredients and continue until the mixture has a creamy consistency.

IV Day
Peach and berries

• 2 handfuls of kale leaves • 1 handful of spinach • 2 cups of water • 2 peeled and cored apples • ½ cup of peeled and chopped peaches • ½ cup of mixed berries • 2 sachets of sweetener based of stevia • 2 tablespoons of flaxseed powder

Optional: 1 scoop of protein powder

Blend the kale leaves and spinach in the water until you get a green juice. Add the remaining ingredients and continue until the mixture has a creamy consistency.

5th day
Spinach, peach and mixed fruits

• 3 handfuls of spinach • 2 cups of water • 1 cup of peeled and chopped peaches • 1 handful of seedless grapes • ½ cup of blueberries • 3 sachets of stevia based sweetener • 2 tablespoons of seeds flax powder

Optional: 1 scoop of protein powder

Blend the spinach in the water until you get a green juice. Add the remaining ingredients and continue until the mixture has a creamy consistency.

6th day
Pineapple and spinach

• 2 handfuls of spinach • 2 cups of water • 1 cup of peeled and chopped pineapple • 2 cups of peeled and chopped peaches • 2 bananas • ½ sachet of stevia based sweetener • 2 tablespoons of flaxseed dust
Optional: 1 scoop of protein powder Blend the spinach in the water until you get a green juice. Add the remaining ingredients and continue until the mixture has a creamy consistency.

VII Day
Pineapple and mixed fruits

• 2 handfuls of mixed salad • 2 handfuls of spinach • 2 cups of water • 1 banana • ½ cup of peeled and chopped pineapple • ½ cup of peeled and chopped mango • 1 cup of mixed berries • 3 sachets of stevia-based sweetener • 2 tablespoons of flaxseed powder
Optional: 1 scoop of protein powder

Blend the mixed salad and spinach in the water until you get a green juice. Add the remaining ingredients and continue until the mixture has a creamy consistency.

VIII Day
Spinach, kale and blueberry

• 2 handfuls of spinach • 2 handfuls of kale • 2 cups of water • 1 peeled and cored apple • 1 banana • ½ cup of blueberries • 2 sachets of stevia based sweetener • 2 tablespoons of flaxseed powder .

Optional: 1 scoop of protein powder
Blend the kale leaves and spinach in the water until you get a green juice. Add the remaining ingredients and continue until the mixture has a creamy consistency.

IX Day
Apple and mango

• 3 handfuls of spinach • 2 cups of water • 1 peeled and cored apple • ½ cup chopped and peeled mango • 2 cups of strawberries • 1 sachet of stevia based sweetener • 2 tablespoons of flaxseed powder

Optional: 1 scoop of protein powder

Blend the spinach in the water until you get a green juice. Add the remaining ingredients and continue until the mixture has a creamy consistency.

X Day
Pineapple and black cabbage

• 2 handfuls of black cabbage • 1 handful of mixed salad • 2 cups of water • ½ cup of chopped peaches • 2 handfuls of peeled and chopped pineapple • 2 sachets of stevia based sweetener • 2 tablespoons of flax seeds in powder

Optional: 1 scoop of protein powder

Blend the cabbage leaves and the mixed salad in the water until you get a green juice. Add the remaining ingredients and continue until the mixture has a creamy consistency.

7 DAYS 7 SMOOTHIES DETOX

Day 1: Peach smoothie, berries and black cabbage

A handful of kale leaves, berries, a peach and flax seeds, all with brown sugar and a few pieces of apple to give consistency. A creamy smoothie perfect for regaining well-being and health.

Day 2: Green apple and kiwi smoothie

In this smoothie you will have to blend the kiwifruit, whose pulp rich in fiber helps regulate intestinal functions and metabolism and the green apple. All accompanied by a few drops of lime, basil, mint and brown sugar. A fresh, creamy and fragrant smoothie, a must try.

Day 3: Banana, pineapple, spinach and coconut milk smoothie

Here too we use green leaves, which help purify the body, but let's add an exotic touch: banana, coconut milk and pineapple. Blend the spinach in the water until you get a green juice and then add the remaining ingredients; then continue until you get a creamy consistency.

Day 4: Pineapple, peach and spinach smoothie

Here too we find an exotic flavor, but which is sweetened by the presence of peach. Add brown sugar to make your smoothie more delicious or a few slices of banana.

Day 5: Blackberry, blueberry and almond milk smoothie

An excellent smoothie rich in fiber and taste: it is the smoothie based on blackberries and blueberries, which is enriched with flax seeds, chia seeds and almond milk. With this drink you will be able to regularize the intestines and also to fight abdominal swelling.

Day 6: Apple, spinach and blueberry smoothie

We continue with the blueberries, and we find again spinach and apple. The ingredients of this drink are not very sweet, so you can add milk, honey or a teaspoon of brown sugar.

Day 7: Smoothie with melon, banana and matcha tea

Fresh, nutritious, delicious. We end the week with a melon and banana smoothie, which is enriched with almond milk, chia seeds and finally matcha tea powder. This tea, in addition to having no calories, is a strong antioxidant, able to protect the liver from toxins.

MILKSHAKES

Milk drinks have been around since we managed to tame the first cow. However, until the invention of refrigeration, only rudimentary cooling systems were available - ice boxes or ice delivery - and this made storage of fresh milk difficult.

Most milk-based drinks were cooked or served hot. Drinking raw milk was known to be problematic in the past unhygienic due to contamination by Salmonella, E. coli, Listeria, Campylobacter.
The first popular milk-based drinks were posset and syllabub, both dating back to at least the 16th century, but probably much earlier. Flips and eggnog were also famous and, as Jerry Thomas pointed out in Eggnog in 1862, it "has a cosmopolitan popularity" which is a claim still true today.

When the term "milkshake" was first used in print in 1885, milkshakes were a whiskey-based alcoholic beverage that has been described as a "type of robust and healthy drink made from eggnog, with egg, whiskey, etc., served both as a tonic and as a delight ". For this reason, milkshakes were sold, incredibly for our times, in pharmacies.

Over time, syrups and ice cream were then added, up to the milkshake as we know it today, made creamy by the use of the electric blender, even if originally the recipe provided that it was mixed by the force released energetically from the arms. using a shaker.

Even today the most popular "flavors" are the great classics (chocolate, vanilla, strawberry, banana) while the most traditional combination, deriving from the now historical American habits, is the one with french fries.

Salted caramel milkshake and high calorie milkshakes are popular with scorched marshmallows, peanut butter, pancakes, shredded chocolate chip cookies or even caramelized popcorn.

Original milkshake

The original milkshake was a simple, light, frothy concoction that was not loaded with calories.

Preparation time: 3 minutes

Ingredients:

1 oz of flavored syrup
4½ oz of milk to fill the glass
½ oz of light cream (18%)
2 ice cubes
nutmeg

Instructions:

In a shaker, add the milk, cream and flavoring syrup and two medium-sized ice cubes.
Shake well for 2 to 3 minutes until the mixture is no longer noisy
Strain into a 10-ounce glass
Grate over the nutmeg

Tips:

This drink requires a lot of physical effort, but the result is unlike any other drink. It is a light but extremely flavorful drink, similar to whipped cream but not as rich and much more drinkable. It is a low calorie milkshake.

The most popular flavor in the US in the 1980s and 1990s was a blend of vanilla and pineapple flavors.

Peanut butter and chocolate banana milkshake

Ingredients (for 1 milkshake):

30 ml of milk (the milk must be very cold)
a banana (put it in the fridge for about an hour before adding it to the smoothie)
2 tablespoons of vanilla ice cream
2 teaspoons of creamy peanut butter
1 Reese's Peanut Butter cup or 2 mini Reese's cups

Tips:

If you are concerned that the taste of peanut butter is too strong, add a few pieces of chocolate or use only Reese's cups, without adding the peanut butter.

Preparation:

Put all the ingredients in the blender, try not to leave them too far out of the fridge
blend for about a minute, until you get a homogeneous mixture
pour everything into a large glass

Milkshake Oreo

The Oreo milkshake is a great dessert for any occasion, and if you are used to enjoying the more classic strawberry milkshake (the strawberry milkshake), I definitely recommend you try this too and delight your palate. A more full-bodied variant, even if no more caloric than that with strawberries.

Ingredients (for 1 milkshake):

200 gr of ice cream (vanilla)
50 gr of ice cream (cream)
120 ml of milk (whole)
3 Oreo cookies

1 tablespoon of Nutella (or other chocolate cream)
1 teaspoon of vanilla essence

To complete:

to taste of whipped cream
to taste of Oreo cookies

Preparation:

To prepare the Oreo milkshake, start putting vanilla ice cream and cream ice cream, milk, Nutella (or other chocolate spread), a teaspoon of vanilla essence and Oreo cookies in the blender jug. Blend everything until you get a creamy mixture.

When it is ready, pour your milkshake into very tall glasses (the typical milkshake ones) that are very cold, otherwise you risk that the hot glasses will immediately make the milkshake liquid, especially if the outside temperature is very high. Finish by decorating with whipped cream and Oreo cookies.

Strawberry Milkshake

Having mentioned this historic milkshake in the previous recipe, let's now see how to prepare it.

Ingredients:

350 g of fresh strawberries
300 ml of milk
4 tablespoons of sugar
1 tablespoon of strawberry ice cream (optional)
6 or 7 ice cubes

Preparation:

Wash and clean the strawberries, set aside 3 or 4 and cut the others into small pieces and put them in a bowl. Place the bowl in the freezer for a few minutes, then take the strawberries and put them in the blender.
Add the ice, milk and sugar. Finally, add the strawberry ice cream and blend everything. When you get a thick and full-bodied cream, pour it into the glasses that you have cooled in the freezer and garnish them with the strawberries you left aside.

Vegan Chocolate Milkshake

This recipe is an example for the creation of vegan milkshakes by replacing ice cream with soy milk.

Ingredients (for two milkshakes):

250 g frozen almond milk (or chocolate ice cream)
100 g cold almond milk
40 g dark chocolate only if you are not using chocolate ice cream
10 g unsweetened cocoa only if you do not use chocolate ice cream
20 g brown sugar or another sweetener of your choice
1 tsp hazelnut cream

Method:

The day before, pour the milk into the ice mold and store in the freezer.
The next day, or when you decide to prepare the milkshake, pour the frozen milk, the chopped chocolate and all the other ingredients into a powerful mixer and

blend. In order not to overheat the mixer, take breaks.

Blend until you get the desired consistency. According to your tastes, add more milk and sugar. Pour the chocolate milkshake into glasses, decorated with chocolate chips and serve immediately.

14 variants of Milkshake to conclude

Banana milkshake- 1 pint of vanilla ice cream, 1 overripe banana, 1 cup of whole milk, 1/2 tsp. vanilla extract

Salted caramel milkshake- 1 liter French vanilla ice cream, natural caramel sauce, such as King's Cupboard caramel sauce (compare prices), 1 cup whole milk, 1 tsp. sea salt

Mounds Bar Milkshake- 1 liter chocolate ice cream, 1/2 cups whole milk, 1/4 cup flaked coconut, 3 tbsp. chocolate chips

Cherry vanilla milkshake- 1 vanilla cherry ice cream, 1-1 / 2 cups of whole milk, 1/2 cup of pitted dark cherries, 1/2 tsp. vanilla extract

Mexican chocolate milkshake- 1 1 liter chocolate ice cream, 1/2 cups whole milk, 1/4 cup natural chocolate sauce, 1/8 tsp. cayenne pepper

Peanut Butter Milkshake- 1 pint of vanilla ice cream, 1-1 / 2 cups of whole milk, 1/4 cup of creamy peanut butter, 1 tsp. vanilla extract

Mint Oreo Milkshake - 1 liter vanilla ice cream, 1/2 cups whole milk, 4 mint chocolate sandwich cookies

Tiramisu milkshake- 1 coffee ice cream, 2 tbsp. chocolate sauce, 1 tbsp. mascarpone cheese or cream cheese, 1 tsp. cinnamon, chocolate flakes for garnish

Grasshopper milkshake - 1 chocolate ice cream with mint and nugget, 1-1 / 2 cups of whole milk, 4 chocolate cookies with mint and mint (like mint)

Key Lime Pie Milkshake - 1 pint vanilla ice cream, 1 cup whole milk, 1/2 cup Rose key lime juice, 2 graham crackers

Chocolate milkshake with peanut butter - 1 liter chocolate ice cream, 1-1 / 2 cups of whole milk, 2 heaping tablespoons. peanut butter, 2 tbsp. chocolate sauce

Pecan praline milkshake- 1 glass of French vanilla ice cream, 1/4 cups whole milk, 1/4 cup half-cup pecan, 2 tbsp. Brown sugar

Strawberry milkshake dipped in chocolate- 1 chocolate ice cream, 1/2 cup of frozen strawberries, 1-1 / 2 cups of whole milk, 2 tbsp. chocolate chips

Chocolate milkshake with marshmallows- 1 liter chocolate ice cream, 1 cup of whole milk, 1/2 cup of marshmallow fluff, 2 tbsp. chocolate chips

Printed in Great Britain
by Amazon